Hodk....

MW01030809

Suzanne Bloch, lutenist, 1954.

CONTEMPORARY MUSICIANS IN PHOTOGRAPHS

TAKEN AT THE
EASTMAN SCHOOL OF MUSIC
BY
LOUIS OUZER

WITH TEXT BY
FRANCIS CROCIATA

DOVER PUBLICATIONS, INC.
NEW YORK

ACKNOWLEDGMENTS

The photographer-author gratefully acknowledges the assistance and encouragement of these people and institutions in the preparation of this collection: Helen Ouzer, Alec Wilder, Francis Crociata, Robert Freeman, Ruth Watanabe, Richard Freed, Will Moyle, Cliff Smith, Neil Bunker, Tony Dechario, the Eastman School of Music of the University of Rochester and the Rochester Philharmonic Orchestra. Special thanks are also due Merritt Torrey, Jr., and the late Merritt Torrey, Sr., who as stage managers of the Eastman Theatre have been responsible for the author's presence backstage for most of these photos.

With few exceptions, the prints used in the production of this edition were made from the original negatives by Laurence E. Keefe.

L. O.

To Helen, Sandy and Billy

Copyright © 1979 by Louis Ouzer for the photographs.
Copyright © 1979 by Francis Crociata for the text.
All rights reserved under Pan American and International Copyright Conventions.

Published in Canada by General Publishing Company, Ltd., 30 Lesmill Road, Don Mills, Toronto, Ontario.

Published in the United Kingdom by Constable and Company, Ltd., 10 Orange Street, London WC2H 7EG.

Contemporary Musicians in Photographs is a new work, first published by Dover Publications, Inc., in 1979.

International Standard Book Number: 0-486-23859-8
Library of Congress Catalog Card Number: 79-54808

Manufactured in the United States of America
Dover Publications, Inc.
180 Varick Street
New York, N.Y. 10014

INTRODUCTION

"Chances are, I'm the oldest—and probably the worst—student at the Eastman School. For fifty years my camera and I have roamed the halls and classrooms without once completing a course or even learning to read music." In this way photographer Louis Ouzer (Fig. 1) describes a five-decade love affair with two venerable musical institutions, both neatly gathered behind a handsome stone facade at the corner of East Main and Gibbs Streets in downtown Rochester, New York.

These institutions are the Eastman Theatre and the Eastman School of Music of the University of Rochester. Planned and financed by the noted inventor and philanthropist George Eastman, founder of the Eastman Kodak Company, they have, as their founder envisioned at their respective openings in 1921 and 1923, brought to Rochester the world's celebrated musical artists.

FIG. 1. Louis Ouzer, 1978. Photo by Laurence E. Keefe.

Louis Ouzer, born in Rochester in 1913 of Russian-Jewish parentage, was introduced to the world behind Eastman's stone facade while he, the School and the Theatre were all young. He was in the third year of what he frankly describes as an unhappy and unsuccessful course of studies at Thomas A. Edison Technical High School, when photography and music entered his life, both resident in the person of Joseph Schiff. A neighbor and family friend, Schiff was a member of the viola section of the Rochester Philharmonic Orchestra and, like most of his colleagues, he "moonlighted" to make ends meet. His other profession was that of a commercial studio photographer and his business had grown so that he needed a part-time darkroom lab assistant, which job he offered to Lou.

An immediate and positive change was evident in the boy. A speech impediment of considerable severity disappeared almost completely. Ouzer describes his work in Schiff's darkroom as therapeutic, so much so in fact that his interest in completing his high-school studies waned completely. Finally Schiff was able to persuade a sympathetic guidance counselor to create a spontaneous pilot work-study program allowing Lou to learn the technical aspects of photographic processes as Schiff's apprentice.

From the earliest years of portrait photography, musical artists have been high among the celebrated public figures most frequently sought as subjects. It is natural then for a number of archives of musical portraiture to be assembled in Rochester, a city noted not only for its musical life, but especially for the production of photographic and optical products. Preceding Ouzer in documenting the world of classical music and jazz as seen in the halls and theaters of the Eastman buildings were his teacher, Schiff, and violinists Alexander Leventon and Brian Morgan. Unlike Ouzer, their work, undertaken during the 1920s and 30s, was done under studio conditions. They either persuaded the artist to visit their studio or hauled their bulky, large-format equipment to the theater dressing rooms or the artists' hotel suites. While their achievements were considerable, as evidenced by a number of memorable published formal portraits of artists like Rachmaninoff, Reiner,

Paderewski and Kreisler, their portfolios contained but a handful of the several hundred artists who visited Eastman during those early years.

It was during these excursions to the theater, following behind Schiff and carrying his cameras and light stands, that Ouzer became fascinated with the idea of capturing great artists in unfamiliar settings, especially in the time and space between the dressing room and the stage. A coincidental interest in the potentials of available-light photography, along with his natural shyness, which precluded making elaborate arrangements for formal portrait sittings, were the contributing factors to the formation of Ouzer's unique style. He was determined to make minimal demands on the time and attention of his artist subjects, but was unrelenting in demands on his own steady hands and especially his printmaking craft.

For over a decade Ouzer had been content to work as Schiff's lab assistant. However, encouraged by several friends he had made at Eastman in the early 1930s, especially composer-lyricist Alec Wilder, who has remained close to Ouzer and his family ever since, Ouzer bought a second-hand Leica 35mm from Joseph Shale, the local Steinway piano dealer, and began experimenting in abstract photography. In 1940 he approached Fritz Kreisler, asking if he might take a few frames backstage before the start of Kreisler's recital. The result was the Kreisler portrait included in this volume (page 15), taken in the dimly lit corridor outside Kreisler's dressing room. This was the first of what would eventually grow to be a collection of several thousand musicians at work and at rest.

After serving in an Army Intelligence photo unit in England and France, Ouzer returned to Schiff's studio and acquired it, along with his mentor's collection of negatives, upon Schiff's death in 1946. He established himself as a commercial photographer specializing in nearly everything—weddings and bar mitzvahs, studio work for advertising media, and especially free-lance photojournalism. In this last context, Ouzer's work has appeared in *Life*, *Newsweek*, *Business Week*, *U.S. News and World Report*, the *New York Times*, and the *Encyclopaedia Britannica*. The reference work used a picture selected from a major Ouzer photo essay on the race riots in Rochester during the summer of 1963. Several of his photos were selected for Pearl S. Buck's *The Joy of Children*, and an important photo essay on Jerusalem immediately following the 1967 Arab-Israeli War, a collaboration with his friend and fellow journalist Rev. Henry Atwell, appeared in many American sectarian publications.

Pressed to identify his favorite occupation, Ouzer prefers his role as a free-lance photojournalist above all others. As such he has photographed innumerable bank presidents in boardrooms, has climbed utility poles to photograph cable splicers at work, has seemingly concelebrated high Roman Catholic liturgical ceremonies with Archbishop Fulton J. Sheen, and above all, has chronicled the life and times of a great music conservatory. Although he has never enjoyed a formal relationship with Eastman's institutions, he has always managed his business and private life to accommodate them as his favorite clients. The studio that he acquired from Schiff was but a few blocks away from the School. Ouzer moved it only once, to a shop on Gibbs Street, just three doors away from the School's vaulted main corridor.

One of the permanent Rochester musical personalities who appears most frequently in Ouzer's collection is Howard Hanson, the Pulitzer Prize-winning composer and conductor who directed the School for forty years until his retirement in 1964. In this collection he is represented in a portrait taken on the set of a 1977 production of his Nathaniel Hawthorne-inspired opera *Merry Mount* (page 47). More recently, Ouzer was called to cover a late-night recording session in the School's Kilbourn Hall, presided over by the still active and vibrant octogenarian composer. The orchestra was comprised of advanced Eastman instrumental students, and the music included the few Hanson compositions that had somehow managed to escape the recorded repertoire of Eastman's orchestras. Ouzer has covered hundreds of occasions of this kind, but nevertheless was totally surprised when Dr. Hanson broke the intense concentration of the recording session to introduce his old friend and colleague to this latest generation of young musical artists, adding: "You needn't worry about his shutter making noise; Lou only clicks on the downbeats!"

In all likelihood, the students in Hanson's orchestra saw the photos from that session within a few days in the ever-changing window exhibit of Ouzer's studio, arranged solely for the delight of passing musicians and theater patrons.

During the late 1960s, when the School approached its fiftieth-anniversary celebration, the School's publicist, Richard Freed, asked Lou to make a selection of his favorite photos for inclusion in a specially prepared desk calendar. Though that collection did include a few of the celebrated artists who also appear in this book, it was mainly a more anonymous collection of students, buildings and instruments—but especially students, in whose faces can be seen reflected the inspiration they derived from the personalities they had come to Rochester to hear and to learn from. That little calendar was so

FIG. 2. Rudolf Serkin, pianist, 1974.

enthusiastically received that Freed immediately began encouraging Lou to survey his whole collection of celebrated classical and jazz musicians and teachers with a view to publication, a request that I renewed during three wonderful years as one of Freed's successors. Lou and I began sifting through his file of negatives during the summer of 1976. I recall he suggested that we might find a maximum of forty or perhaps fifty photographs and subjects. He was genuinely astounded, after more than a year of organizing and editing, to realize that he would have to select from more than three hundred subjects. The selection process would be even more painful since so many of the subjects were also his friends.

Few photographs in his collection need any explanation. In every instance where the artist subject is not a household name to the general concert-going public, he is a legend within the professional music world, and especially among orchestral musicians. Although these less famous sitters were all distinguished composers or performers, it was their achievement as teachers that set them apart from their colleagues. They include artists like Oscar Zimmerman (page 26), who was Toscanini's first principal bass in the N.B.C. Symphony before leaving in

1946 to teach at Eastman and perform in the Rochester Philharmonic Orchestra; flutist Joseph Mariano (page 32), who is represented by students in nearly every major symphony orchestra in the United States; and the legendary trombone professor Emory Remington ("the Chief"; page 35), whose fame as a pedagogue spread literally around the world. When the Leningrad Philharmonic visited Rochester on their first American tour in 1963, their first words to the press on stepping out of the tour bus were: "Where Remington?"

As Lou made this selection, he would occasionally recall an especially charming comment or touching circumstance, especially in connection with photos taken backstage moments before or after a performance. The sliver of light illuminating the profile of pianist Rudolf Serkin (Fig. 2) is a reflection of the Eastman Theatre's houselights as he peeks through the curtains (counting the house?). The temperature onstage is comfortable, but Glenn Gould, rehearsing with the Rochester Philharmonic, is wrapped in several sweaters and is wearing fingerless practice gloves (page 3). Vladimir Horowitz is reliving in mime for his manager a particularly visual passage he has just played onstage (page 4). Violinist-

FIG. 3. Alec Wilder, composer, 1972.

educator Shinichi Suzuki is coaching a group of children as they confront the violin for the first time (page 117). (In a companion frame, the single Oriental child in the group is the only one who immediately tucks the fiddle under her chin, striking a virtuoso pose.) The poignant photo of Marian Anderson (page 40) was taken as she sat alone watching a group of newsmen and photographers crowded around New York State Governor Thomas E. Dewey. Winthrop Sargeant and Olin Downes, known to millions as byline music reviewers in the *New Yorker* and the *New York Times*, are seen occupying seats in Kilbourn Hall listening to a performance (page 115). And how many on seeing Karl Haas's photo taken during a lecture (page 116) will be for the first time matching the face to the voice that dominates the most widely syndicated classical radio program?

It has always been one of Ouzer's special treats to see one of his portrait subjects—especially an artist returning to the venerable hotel located around the corner from the theater—stop in front of his studio, first astonished and then delighted to see a display of beautifully printed and mounted photographs of the day's rehearsal or master class. The artist had probably not even noticed Ouzer at work. Nearly always he will enter the shop to be greeted by Ouzer's effervescent wife Helen (his childhood sweetheart), and

after a few moments of Ouzer's hospitality—highlighted recently by a showing of prints being selected for this volume—he will leave with a gift of prints of the kind that no formal portrait sitting could ever produce.

You are likely to see an Ouzer print in just about any setting where a musician or music lover lives or works. The making of his musical portraits has already rewarded him with thousands of friends. Ouzer's generosity is the point of a passage from Alec Wilder's personal memoir, *Letters I Never Mailed*: "You are the last on this list of beautiful souls who have kept their own counsel, stuck to their own vision, followed their own star . . . how you've managed to give away so many thousands of photographs I shall never know. But you have." (Portraits of Wilder appear in Fig. 3 and on page 112.)

In the foreword to that 1971 Eastman calendar containing his earlier collection, Ouzer supplied this answer to his friend's question: "I hope the dynamic idealism of these beautiful people is reflected in this portfolio—a tiny fraction of the thousands of prints that clutter my studio. I hope that they afford others a portion of the pleasure that taking them has given me."

FRANCIS CROCIATA

Arthur Rubinstein, pianist, 1964.

José Iturbi, pianist, 1962.

Glenn Gould, pianist, 1957.

Harold Shaw, impresario; Vladimir Horowitz, pianist, 1978.

Robert Casadesus, pianist, 1959.

Vladimir Ashkenazy, pianist, 1972.

Alicia de Larrocha, pianist, 1974.

André Watts, pianist, 1966.

Rudolf Serkin, pianist, 1972.

David Burge, pianist; George Crumb, composer, 1976.

Igor Kipnis, harpsichordist, 1976.

E. Power Biggs, organist, 1970.

David Craighead, organist, 1975.

Yehudi Menuhin, violinist, 1965.

Fritz Kreisler, violinist-composer, 1940.

Itzhak Perlman, violinist, 1970.

Alexander Schneider, violinist-conductor, 1973.

David Oistrakh, violinist-conductor, 1970.

Isaac Stern, violinist, 1972.

Eastman String Quartet: John Celentano, Joseph Knitzer, violins; Francis Bundra, viola; Georges Miquelle, cello, 1960.

Henryk Szeryng, violinist, 1971.

William Primrose, Francis Tursi, violists, 1977.

Walter Trampler, violist, 1977.

Mstislav Rostropovich, cellist-conductor, 1971.

Leonard Rose, cellist, 1978.

Oscar Zimmerman, double bassist, 1966.

Janos Starker, cellist, 1973.

Julian Bream, lutenist, 1970.

Mitch Miller, oboist-conductor, 1969.

Jean-Pierre Rampal, flutist-conductor, 1973.

James Galway, Julius Baker, flutists, 1975.

Joseph Mariano, flutist, 1966.

John Barrows, French horn, 1967.

Harvey Phillips, tuba, 1970.

Emory Remington, trombonist, 1970.

Kiko Abe, marimbist-composer, 1977.

Jennie Tourel, mezzo-soprano, 1969.

Marilyn Horne, mezzo-soprano, 1972.

Joan Sutherland, soprano, 1975.

Marian Anderson, contralto, 1957.

Jan Peerce, tenor, 1969.

Leontyne Price, soprano, 1973.

Jan DeGaetani, mezzo-soprano, 1978.

Lauritz Melchior, tenor, 1942.

Michael Tilson Thomas, conductor; Beverly Sills, soprano, 1971.

William Warfield, bass-baritone, 1961.

Howard Hanson, composer-conductor, 1976.

Warren Benson, composer, 1970.

Krzysztof Penderecki, composer, 1972.

Peter Mennin, composer, 1967.

Henry Cowell, composer, 1960.

Aram Khachaturian, composer, 1968.

Igor Stravinsky, composer-conductor, 1966.

Robert Russell Bennett, composer, 1957.

Aaron Copland, composer-conductor, 1976.

Gunther Schuller, composer-conductor, 1970.

George Rochberg, composer, 1974.

Bruno Maderna, composer, 1972.

Elliott Carter, composer, 1976.

Anton Heiller, organist-composer, 1968.

Vincent Persichetti, composer, 1974.

Carlos Chávez, composer-conductor, 1970.

David Diamond, composer, 1968.

Lukas Foss, composer-conductor, 1974.

Pierre Boulez, composer-conductor, 1974.

Frederick Fennell, conductor, 1956.

Erich Leinsdorf, conductor, 1952.

Sarah Caldwell, conductor, 1976.

Pierre Monteux, conductor, 1959.

Antal Dorati, conductor, 1967.

Walter Hendl, conductor, 1971.

Julius Rudel, conductor, 1973.

David Zinman, conductor, 1973.

Henry Lewis, conductor, 1972.

Leopold Stokowski, conductor, 1965.

Karel Husa, composer-conductor, 1973.

Dimitri Mitropoulos, conductor, 1950.

Charles Munch, conductor, 1957.

Evgeny Svetlanov, conductor, 1970.

Duke Ellington, composer-pianist, 1965.

Bill Evans, composer-pianist, 1977.

Erroll Garner, composer-pianist, 1961.

Count Basie, composer-pianist, 1975.

Dave Brubeck, composer-pianist.

Oscar Peterson, composer-pianist, 1976.

Keith Jarrett, composer-pianist, 1976.

Marian McPartland, composer-pianist, 1970.

Mike Moore, bassist; Gene Bertoncini, guitarist, 1976.

Joe Venuti, violinist, 1975.

Jack Benny, comedian-violinist, and Millard Taylor, concertmaster, 1959.

Ron Carter, bassist, 1974.

Stéphane Grappelli, violinist, 1974.

Woody Herman, clarinetist, 1974.

Herb Hall, clarinetist, 1976.

Dizzy Gillespie, trumpeter, 1972.

Louis Armstrong, trumpeter, 1956.

Vic Dickenson, trombonist, 1976.

Thad Jones, trumpeter, 1973.

Phil Woods, saxophonist, 1977.

Oliver Nelson, saxophonist, 1972.

100

Stan Getz, saxophonist, 1974.

Jimmy McPartland, trumpeter, 1976.

Gerry Mulligan, saxophonist, 1973.

Mel Torme, singer, 1968.

Joe Williams, singer, 1976.

Ella Fitzgerald, singer, 1966.

Lena Horne, singer, 1956.

Tony Bennett, singer, 1973.

Paul Desmond, saxophonist, 1971.

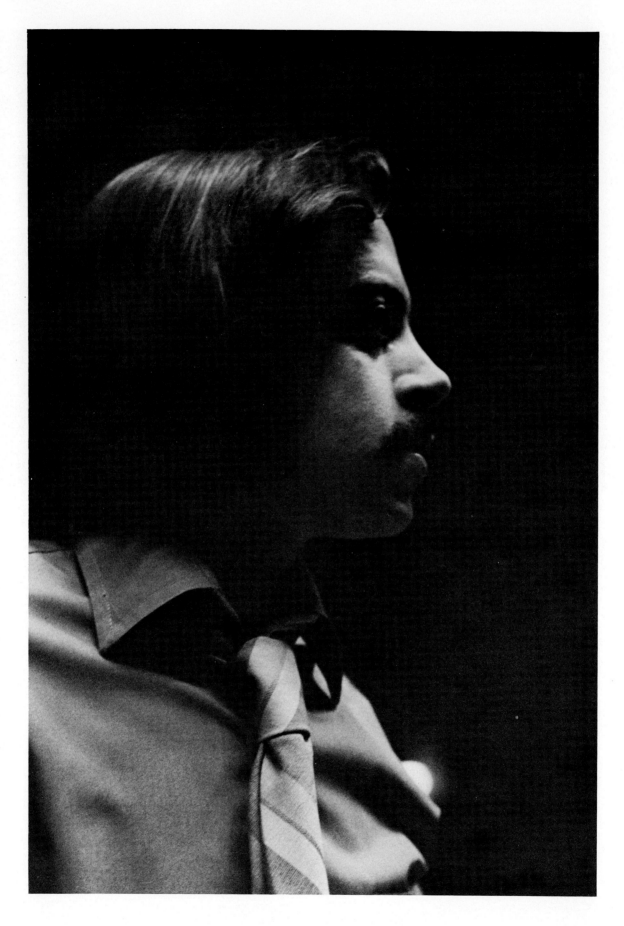

Chuck Mangione, flügelhorn, 1970.

Harold Arlen, composer-pianist, 1973.

Alec Wilder, composer, 1967.

Michel Legrand, composer-pianist, 1976.

Harold C. Schonberg, music critic-historian, 1979.

Olin Downes, Winthrop Sargeant, music critics, 1955.

Karl Haas, conductor-lecturer, 1977.

Shinichi Suzuki, violinist-educator, 1966.

H. C. Robbins Landon, musicologist, 1972.

INDEX